Low-Carb Gluten-Free
Yeast Bread Recipes
to Slim By

Low-Carb Gluten-Free
Yeast Bread Recipes
to Slim By

By

Em Elless

Book and Cover Design by M.L. Smith

MUFN Books™

Low-Carb Gluten-Free
Yeast Bread Recipes
to Slim By

Volume Two of
"to Slim By" series

Contact: editor@mufnbooks.com

ISBN #978-0-9858224-3-9

Library of Congress Control Number: 2013954139

Table of Contents

Low-Carb Gluten-Free Yeast Bread Recipes to Slim By

Introduction

S uppose you want to build a better, stronger house but for a number of important reasons you cannot use most of the standard construction materials – no wood of any variety, no wood byproducts, no nails, no staples, no starch adhesives, no drywall, no Styrofoam – *none* of the commonplace products used for centuries to build houses. This means all standard blueprints are off the table as well. What you have in mind changes the very foundation of what many believe is the only right way to build a house.

The good news is, several new products have come on the market that are promoted as wonderful substitutes. The bad news is, after examining what they are made of, you learn that many of them create a more vulnerable house than the materials you are trying to avoid.

You gather together the few remaining products you can use: stone, cement, metal and steel, adobe, bamboo (which is a grass), nuts and bolts. Your house is going to cost more to build but it will be much more energy efficient. You will recover your money in a short time in lower utility bills – and you won't have the expense of ongoing repairs. You will have a strong house that will help protect you and your family for decades.

Creating low-carb gluten-free yeast bread is an entirely different and challenging concept. It goes against everything we ever knew and been told we must to do to create a good loaf of bread. There is no gluten for yeast to feast on; no wonderful puffy mound of dough to punch down to rise again, tastier and chewier; no cups of sugar, tenderizing and caramelizing.

Instead of kneading we must whip.

Instead of rolling out, we spoon or pour.

Instead of watching dough rise two or three times, it is the nature of low-carb bread to rise once, and then bake.

Instead of five pound bags of inexpensive flour, we must use one pound bags of unconventional ingredients that are healthful and delicious, but definitely pricier: finely ground nuts, beans and seeds; powdered coconut; whey or other protein powders.

But they work, and combined in the right way with the right ingredients they create delicious breads that not only rival their carbohydrate-rich counterparts in flavor, they far-and-away surpass them in protein, fiber and nutrients – and low carbs! The following recipes cost more to prepare, but the payoff in our health, well-being and quality of life is much more valuable.

The phrase "low-carb gluten-free" has been an oxymoron because most gluten-free products used in bread-making are very high in refined carbohydrates (starches and sugars), many of them much worse than the wheat flours they are replacing. Sorghum flour, potato flour, brown and white rice flours, etc. and *all* the starches spike blood sugar levels to diabetic or pre-diabetic levels, can escalate hypertension, inflammation and heart disease – and pile on the pounds.

When I gathered together the primary products that are lowest in carbs and highest in nutrients, I had a total of five to work with: almond flour; coconut flour; ground flaxseed, white bean flour (the highest carbs but also high in fiber and protein) and natural whey protein powder. Hemp (I didn't know how green bread and ham would go over), sunflower and hazelnut flours are also good products but harder to find, so I included them as substitute options.

Most of my early experiments were bombs, literally. Many loaves ended with a thud into the wastebasket, too hard even for the birds to eat (they wouldn't – I tried it). Loaves that weren't quite right but still eatable began to fill the freezer. When it couldn't hold any more I ate bread for breakfast, lunch and dinner – bread too damp or crumbly or flavorless, but okay with lots of butter and a glass of wine. I went through more than 5 pounds of yeast and untold pounds of flour searching for solutions.

More than once I considered abandoning gluten-free and using just enough vital wheat gluten to at least get the loaves in the ballpark of yeast breads. I tried variations of Xanthan gum, unflavored gelatin and egg whites to replace the gluten (necessary to bind the ingredients and create stretchy pockets for yeast to expand) and finally determined that egg whites – lots of them - were the key.

Back in the day when most angel food cakes were made from scratch, it was a delicate job carefully cracking and separating yolk from white into two bowls. If a sliver of gold escaped into the whites it had to be fished out, the slippery thing darting away from the spoon (whites won't whip well with even a trace of yolk or oil).

But now, thanks to pasteurized liquids and powders that are economical and easy to use, we can quickly create voluminous clouds with the help of a little cream of tartar.

I purchase powdered egg whites in a 36 ounce container, the equivalent of 255 egg whites, using just 2 teaspoons of powder for each white. It is also nice having them on hand as a back-up food supply.

I also buy cartons of liquid egg whites at Costco that have a fairly long refrigeration life, and most local groceries sell liquid egg whites in 1 quart containers (compare prices!).

Frothed or whipped, when combined with fragrant flours, wonderful loaves of rich dark pumpernickel or feather-light rolls are created. I served several recipes incognito to family and friends and all received great compliments – followed by shock when I revealed they weren't made with wheat flour.

After "Muffins to Slim By" was published I received several questions asking how to make the recipes adaptable for nut and dairy allergies. I kept these concerns in mind as I developed the yeast bread recipes and provided some substitutes, but could not test every possible alternative.

All products can be problematic for some people. Some will have a blood sugar spike eating caraway seed, others can't tolerate certain sugar-free sweeteners. Where possible I have added the option to use your preferred ingredients and the choice to use or not use others.

Exchanging seed for nut flours may affect the texture, depending how fine the seed is ground, but you should still achieve a wonderful loaf of bread.

Dairy substitutes presented a much bigger challenge. I concluded there was no easy exchange without reworking the recipes, which I may do in another book. My goal for this book was to stay within the limited ingredients chosen for their low carbs and high nutrients.

If you want to substitute ingredients already in your pantry - potato starch for whey protein or sorghum flour for coconut flour – keep in mind that this will dramatically increase carbohydrates and keep you on the same-old-same-old unhealthy treadmill. I encourage you to experiment and discover wonderful new recipes perfect for your body and situation, but do the math. Breads and muffins "to slim by" only help with weight loss when part of a complete low carb diet.

Until manufacturers catch up, we need to create some pans out of foil or tweak what is available. As of this writing the only hot dog or hamburger bun mold pans on the market are commercial sized; none can be found for French-style loaves that are enclosed on each end to support low-carb batters. We must refine some products to make them better suited for fine-textured baking. We must study every label.

We must also – and this may be the hardest - unlearn old habits. No preheating the oven; low-carb flours will brown too quickly before they are fully baked. No more pinches of this and scoops of that because we're experienced hands in the kitchen – the art of low-carb bread-making must be precise. No proofing yeast before it's added to the dough – it has so little to eat it must do what we need it to do inside the bread; remember, there is only enough energy for one rise.

Low-carb gluten-free bread is recent history. There is still so much to explore and learn. It is an exciting process for those of us who know the challenge is worth the effort. New products are being developed every day, often in our own kitchens. Have fun. If you discover a good noodle, let me know.

Em Elless

Important Things to Know: Ingredients

Enjoying our daily bread should be more than having something to wrap around a hamburger, fill a hunger or satisfy a craving with empty calories. Bread can now be part of our daily nutrition goals. If we're going to spend hard-earned money on pricier ingredients, it is important knowing where they come from, what they contribute and how they help us. Here are the major players, and a few minor:

White Bean Flour has a mild, smooth nutty flavor and fortifies our short list of useable flours. It contains a unique kind of fiber called resistant starch, which means that unlike refined starches that practically melt into our bloodstreams, it passes through the small intestine mostly as undigested fiber. It promotes digestive health by encouraging the growth of good bacteria and helps regulate blood sugar because the energy is released later in the large intestine, preventing sudden spikes and decreases between meals. Other important byproducts of this flour's digestive process are compounds called "short chain fatty acids," which help prevent colon cancer by hindering the absorption of carcinogens. Compared with the following flours it contains the most carbohydrates, but the benefits are more than worthwhile.

Natural Whey Protein Powder of course isn't flour at all but for our purpose it is a great replacement. Whey is the liquid that remains after the first stages of cheese production, processed into a concentrated powder. It is considered a complete protein and contains all nine essential amino acids. Studies show that in addition to improving muscle strength (muscle burns more calories), these acids help prevent heart disease, diabetes and age-related bone loss. The list goes on – from anti-cancer properties to improving immune response in children with asthma. It must be supplemented with our other flours but it dissolves quickly to help create delicious nutrient-rich baked goods. 100% natural unflavored whey protein can be found in health food sections online and can be more economical than other brands sold in the grocery department. It is worthwhile comparing prices. Look for products with no additives.

Coconut Flour is naturally 75% fiber in composition, containing 9-10 grams per 2 tablespoons, which reduces the absorption of sugar into the blood stream. It is produced from grinding the dried white internal meat of the coconut. It is also somewhat tricky to work with, absorbing eggs and oil – whatever is wet – like an insatiable sponge, soaking up liquids until it is a saturated clump of porridge. Hence, it cannot be easily tweaked without adjusting the liquids, generally an equal measurement of water or other liquid. This may have a domino effect on the other ingredients. It is best to follow the measurement exactly until you are familiar enough to experiment with exchanges. Coconut flour is not a significant source of protein in bread recipes but contains lauric acid with antiviral and antifungal properties. Its fragrant, smooth, mildly sweet nature adds a unique element even though small amounts are used. It also has the wonderful quality of satisfying our hunger longer.

Golden Flaxseed Meal comes from a delicate wildflower with pure, light blue blossoms. The fruit is a small pod that contains tiny, glossy seeds packed with omega-3 fatty acids, antioxidants, fiber, minerals and essential vitamins. It is the only flour to have 0 net carbs (after subtracting the grams of fiber from the same number of carbohydrates) and has a long list of medicinal uses. One important discovery I made is that the texture of the bread is much improved if the meal is further refined in the blender.

The meal on the right with sparkling fragments came directly from the bag and is the finest grind currently available. The meal on the left was processed for 30 seconds in the blender into a light tan, "floury" grind that makes a noticeable improvement in the finished bread.   I refer to it as "refined" in the recipes. Process only ½ cup at a time to prevent overheating and clumping.

Occasionally I come across concerns regarding four potential health issues if large amounts of flaxseed are consumed. Numerous studies, however, report little or no problems from eating it and to the contrary, list many benefits.   Three cyanogenic glycosides contained in flaxseed – also present in broccoli, kale and cabbage, among others – no longer exist when it is baked. Another study reported that a person would need to consume more than 8 cups a day to cause toxicity.   Most of the following recipes that list ground flaxseed use only ½ cup for the entire loaf; two list 1 cup, which averages out to about 2 tablespoons of flaxseed in two servings. I believe that too much of any good thing can cause problems. I would also not recommend eating flax seeds whole, from a digestion standpoint.   If you would still rather substitute one of the other flours, you may have the best success with almond meal, very finely ground.

Ground flaxseed is a wonderful source of vital nutrients and adds a delicious nutty flavor to baked goods. Nutritionally both the golden and dark varieties are the same.

Almond Flour is simply finely ground whole blanched almonds (no skin), rich in vitamins and minerals, high in protein and fiber. Almond *meal* is more the consistency of cornmeal. Some almond flour brands are more coarsely ground, which affects the texture. In dense or quick-type breads this doesn't really matter, but when we're trying to achieve a more tender crumb – white bread, Challah, French-style – the appearance and sensory response are important. Look for products that indicate they are very finely ground. They cost more, but you will be happier with the finished bread.

EGG WHITES: As I wrote in the Introduction, even a large number of egg whites in a recipe is fairly inexpensive and easy to prepare. I buy them two ways; in powder form in a 36 ounce canister that equals 255 whites, and; in liquid form which can be purchased very economically in warehouse stores like Costco or 1 quart cartons in local groceries. I have seen wide variations in price so be sure to compare. Because they are pasteurized they won't whip nearly as well as fresh whites, but adding cream of tartar will create beautiful, fluffy mounds just as high as using fresh eggs.

Egg whites are primarily 90% water and 10% proteins, which are long chains of amino acids. When we whip air into the whites these chains become denatured, which means they unravel and stretch into shapes that trap air, creating light textures in what we bake. There is a notion floating around that cooking/heating protein - which includes protein powders like whey – destroys the nutritional value because our bodies can't absorb "denatured" foods. This is nonsense. If that were the case we would have to eat everything raw. Eggs, meat, everything we cook and bake is denatured when heated. The food comes out of the oven changed in appearance, but the protein isn't harmed; instead of being wrapped into tight balls, the protein chains become long strands. Cooked or raw, our bodies absorb the same essential amino acids.

Understanding what denaturing really is allows us to enjoy many healthful foods, unhindered by silly arguments.

Xanthan Gum: No gluten-free flour, or any combination thereof, can duplicate the elasticity, binding and gas-holding qualities of gluten. It does magical things, kneaded and stretched, creating delightfully chewy, airy bread. Unfortunately it makes many of us sick. So what are our alternatives? Egg whites are a big help but something more is needed to achieve the texture and suppleness we're looking for.

We have three primary gluten-replacement options: gums – xanthan and guar; ground seeds like flax and chia that become gelatinous when water is added, and; gelatin itself, unflavored. The breads I made with both gelatin and jellied seeds rose and baked all right, but the texture was strange – it reminded me of corrugated paper. Some loaves came out gummy and others collapsed a few hours later into puckered globs. There may be a winning combination but I didn't find it and I finally gave up, unwilling to condemn one more loaf to the trash (I could not eat them, even with wine).

Xanthan is the by-product of a fermentation process when bacteria are introduced to a sugar source, typically derived from corn, wheat, or soy. Many people on gluten-free diets are afraid to use it, believing it may contain elements of gluten protein. But sugar from whatever source does not contain protein. The final end product, Xanthan gum, is a totally new creation – it contains no properties of the sugar it was grown on. If you avoid it because you think it is a corn or wheat product, it isn't. I may be belaboring this, but it would be unfortunate to reject a good product for properties it doesn't possess. Discuss this with your doctor and if you still have misgivings, you may have much better success with the alternatives than I did. There are many combinations I didn't try.

Honey is necessary to provide food for yeast since the flours don't contain sugars to eat or starches to convert into glucose. You can use regular sugar if you prefer; only 1 tablespoon is used for the entire recipe and divided into 8, 12 or 16 servings, our portion is miniscule.

According to the American Diabetes Association white sugar raises blood sugar slightly faster than honey, which has a glycemic range between 31 and 78 depending on the variety.   Locust honey, for instance, has a GI of 32; clover honey has 69. You can research this further on online sites like the Glycemic Index Database. Local raw honey also appears to help seasonal allergies since the bees collect area pollen which helps build your immunity.

I purchase **ACTIVE DRY YEAST** in economical 2 pound packages and store it in a zip-lock bag in the freezer. It only takes a couple minutes for 1 tablespoon of granules to warm to room temperature. I measure it directly from the freezer, (promptly returning it), often adding it to the bowl of dry ingredients without proofing (letting it dissolve and activate into a foam before adding to the recipe).

Yeast production today is so reliable, proofing is only necessary if it is past the expiration date and you need to test whether it is still good. It will activate when it comes in contact with the liquid ingredients in the mixing process.

There is only one rise with low-carb bread. This is my theory only, but since yeast has so little to eat – basically just a tablespoon of honey – I don't want it generating all of its energy in a separate dish; I want its work to start inside the dough. I tested this, one loaf with proofed yeast added and the other with the yeast entering the batter dry; the second loaf rose higher. All brand name packages of yeast sold in North America are gluten-free with the exception of brewer's yeast used in beer production.

Stevia/Sweetener: Many artificial sweeteners and "sugar free" products on the market contain fillers such as dextrose or maltodextrin. These can raise blood sugar just as much as real sugar. I prefer 100% stevia powders. The brand I use is Kal. I also prefer EZ-Sweetz drops as it seems to me to have the least bitter aftertaste but you should use your favorite brand. Each has a different unit of measuring: teaspoons, drops, a packet, or a tiny scoop, so go by "equal to" the measurement.

Note on Nutrition/Carb Information: The calculations I list with each recipe are based on standard products I use which are readily available. It is important to read labels and compare brands! The difference you will find in carbs, fiber, sugars, "fillers" etc. can vary widely and thus your carb totals may differ. I did not factor sweeteners into my totals as everyone has their own preference, so you will need to add in the data, if any, for the product you use.

TWO SPECIAL INGREDIENTS

Diastatic Malt Powder has long been a secret of professional bakers. Although only 1 teaspoon is added to each of the following recipes, it adds significant flavor and a savory home-baked bread aroma. It is listed as an optional ingredient for gluten-free diets because it is made from sprouted grains (usually barley) that have been dried and ground. Fortunately gluten-free varieties of malt and malt substitutes are also being developed and are available on a limited basis. Search online for "malt extract substitute."

"Diastatic" refers to the enzymes that are created as the grain sprouts, which convert starches into sugars and promote yeast growth. I have been unable to determine if these enzymes break down the resistant starches found in white bean flour; I only know the taste and texture is noticeably improved and the bread stays fresh longer. It comes in a 1 pound bag that is relatively inexpensive because only 1 teaspoon is used per loaf. I've made countless dozens and am still using the first bag I purchased. *Note: Do not confuse this with non-diastatic, which is simply a sweetener with no enzymes.*

Deli-Rye Flavor is another product that packs an incredible amount of flavor into just 1 teaspoon of powder. It compensates beautifully for not using rye flour and can be purchased online. If you love pumpernickel and rye bread, it is worth the small investment as it will flavor many, many loaves. It does contain wheat so if you can't tolerate even a trace, there is a gluten-free **Rye Flavor** powder available that can also be purchased online. Opinions seem to go back and forth on this product, whether or not it truly is gluten-free. If you don't want to risk trying it, substitute1 teaspoon of anise extract, 1 teaspoon of dill seed and ½ teaspoon of onion powder - and a little grated orange peel if you would like an added piquancy.

IMPORTANT TIPS

USE AN OVEN THERMOMETER

MOST OVEN TEMPERATURES ARE MUCH HIGHER OR LOWER THAN THE DIAL SETTING.

ALWAYS TEST BREAD FOR DONENESS WITH AN INSTANT READ THERMOMETER

LEVEL DRY INGREDIENTS WITH STRAIGHT EDGE OF A KNIFE OR SPATULA

WARM EGGWHITES BY PLACING CONTAINER IN A BOWL OF HOT TAPWATER
A QUICK WAY TO ALSO WARM WHOLE EGGS

Egg White Conversion Charts

Powdered

1 Egg White	2 tsp. Powder	2 TBS Hot Water
2 Egg Whites	1 TBS + 1 tsp. Powder	¼ Cup Hot Water
3 Egg Whites	2 TBS Powder	¼ Cup + 2 TBS Hot Water
4 Egg Whites	2 TBS + 2 tsp. Powder	½ Cup Hot Water
5 Egg Whites	3 TBS + 1 tsp. Powder	½ Cup + 2 TBS Hot Water
6 Egg Whites	¼ Cup Powder	¾ Cup Hot Water
8 Egg Whites	5 TBS + 1 tsp. Powder	1 Cup Hot Water
10 Egg Whites	6 TBS + 2 tsp. Powder	1 ¼ Cups Hot Water
12 Egg Whites	½ Cup Powder	1 ½ Cups Hot Water

Liquid

1 Egg White	2 TBS Liquid
2 Egg Whites	¼ Cup Liquid
3 Egg Whites	¼ + 2 TBS Liquid
4 Egg Whites	½ Cup Liquid
5 Egg Whites	½ Cup + 2 TBS Liquid
6 Egg Whites	¾ Cup Liquid
8 Egg Whites	1 Cup Liquid
10 Egg Whites	1 ¼ Cups Liquid
12 Egg Whites	1 ½ Cups Liquid

Note: 3 TBS Liquid Egg Whites are approximately equal to 1 whole egg.

Measurement Conversion Chart

1½ teaspoons..	½ Tablespoon
3 teaspoons..	1 Tablespoon
4 teaspoons..	1 Tablespoon + 1 tsp.
½ Tablespoon...	1½ tsp.
1 Tablespoon..	3 tsp.
2 Tablespoons..	⅛ Cup
4 Tablespoons..	¼ Cup
5 Tablespoons + 1 teaspoon...........................	⅓ Cup
8 Tablespoons..	½ Cup
12 Tablespoons...	¾ Cup
16 Tablespoons...	1 Cup
¼ Cup..	4 Tablespoons
⅓ Cup..	5 Tablespoons + 1 tsp.
½ Cup..	8 Tablespoons
¾ Cup..	12 Tablespoons
1 Cup...	16 Tablespoons
⅛ Cup..	2 Tablespoons
⅜ Cup..	¼ Cup + 2 Tablespoons
⅝ Cup..	½ Cup + 2 Tablespoons
⅞ Cup..	¾ Cup + 2 Tablespoons
1⅛ Cup...	1 Cup + 2 Tablespoons
1¼ Cup...	1 Cup + 4 Tablespoons
1 ½ Cup..	1 Cup + 8 Tablespoons

RECIPE LIST

NUTRITION TOTALS:
<u>Entire Loaf</u> - Calories: 1090; Protein: 117 g; Total Carbs: 75 g; Fiber: 34g ; NET CARBS: 42g
<u>1" Thick Slice</u> - Calories: 91; Protein: 10g; Total Carbs: 6.25 g Fiber: 2.8 g NET CARBS: 3.45

Almond Milk and Honey Loaf
Delectable, moist, delicious eaten just plain.
<u>Need: Greased 9" x 5" or 12" bread pan.</u>

ONE:
¾ Cup Unsweetened Almond Milk
1 TBS Butter
1 TBS Honey
1 tsp. Vanilla Extract
6 Drops EZ-Sweetz, *or liquid sweetener equal to 2 TBS*

TWO:
1 Cup Natural Unflavored Whey Protein Powder
½ Cup Flaxseed Flour, *refined to velvety texture in blender*
¼ Cup White Bean Flour
2 TBS. Coconut Flour
1 TBS Active Dry Yeast
2 tsp. Xanthan Gum
1 tsp. Sea Salt
1 tsp. Diastatic Malt Powder, *optional for gluten-free diets*
1 tsp. Baking Powder

THREE:
6 Egg Whites (3/4 Cup), *room temperature*
1 tsp. Cream of Tartar

●In separate dish put **ONE** ingredients. Warm in microwave 1 ½ minutes to melt butter. Stir and set aside.
●In separate bowl put **TWO** ingredients. Blend thoroughly with whisk and set aside.
●In mixer bowl with whisk attachment put **THREE** ingredients, room temperature or slightly warmed if you are working in a cold room. Slowly increase speed to High and whip for 5 minutes, or until a track drawn through whites with a knife-blade doesn't sag.
●Reduce speed to Low/Stir and pour in liquids, then add dry ingredients by spoonsful. When they are all added, stop mixer and remove bowl, knocking any whites clinging to the whisk back into the bowl. Stir by hand with large spoon until whites and dry ingredients are just blended.
●Scoop fluffy batter into pan, set in cold oven, turn on oven light and let rise 1 hour.
●Leaving pan in place, turn on oven to 375° F and bake 30 minutes, or until internal temp is between 190° and 210° F. Remove to cooling rack and baste top with butter.

NUTRITION TOTALS:
Entire Loaf -- Calories: 640; Protein: 64; Total Carbs: 43; Fiber: 17; NET CARBS: 26
1/8 Serving – Calories: 80; Protein: 8 g; Total Carbs: 5g; Fiber: 2 g; NET CARBS: 3 g

Angel Whey Bread

Light and airy with a delectable crust.   <u>Need: Well-greased bread loaf pan</u>

<u>ONE:</u>
½ Cup *Vanilla Whey Protein Powder, *no substitutions*
½ Cup Golden Flaxseed "Flour," *refined to velvety texture in blender*
1 TBS Active Dry Yeast
2 tsp. Xanthan Gum
1 tsp. Sea Salt
1 tsp. Diastatic Malt Powder, *optional for gluten-free diets*

<u>TWO:</u>
8 Egg Whites (1 Cup), *room temperature*
1 tsp. Cream of Tartar
1 TBS Honey

- In separate bowl combine <u>**ONE**</u> ingredients. Blend thoroughly with a whisk and set aside.
- In mixing bowl with whisk attachment put <u>**TWO**</u> Ingredients, *room temperature.* Slowly increase speed to High and whip for five minutes, until track drawn through whites with knife blade doesn't sag.
- Reduce speed to Low/Stir and add dry ingredients by spoonsful.
- Stop mixer, remove bowl and with a large metal spoon slowly fold batter until whites and dry ingredients are just mixed. The finished batter will be billowy. Spoon into a well-greased bread pan; smooth top with spoon. Set pan in cold
- Leaving pan in place, turn oven to 375° F and bake 25-30 minutes, until crust is golden brown and internal temperature is about 200° F. Remove loaf from pan onto cooling rack.

NUTRITION TOTALS - Using ½ loaf of French-Style Bread Recipe, without nuts added
Entire Casserole-- Calories: 1805; Protein: 105.5 g; Total Carbs: 53.5 g ; Fiber: 8g; NET CARBS: 45.5 g
1/12 Serving: Calories: 150   Protein: 9 g   Total Carbs: 4g Fiber: .6g NET CARBS per serving: 4 g

Bread Pudding

<u>Need: Buttered 2 qt. casserole or 8" square baking dish.</u>

This favorite comfort food for many of us is not only possible, it's here – nutritious, low-carb, gluten-free bread pudding! Save leftovers in the freezer from this book's recipes and this delicious dessert is less than an hour away. It is fast and easy to prepare and does not require a hot water bath.

<u>ONE:</u>
Six Rounded Cups of Leftover LC GF Bread
<u>TWO:</u>
1 Cup Almond Milk, *unsweetened*
1 Cup Heavy Whipping Cream
½ Cup Stevia, *or preferred sweetener*
4 Whole Eggs
2 TBS Butter, melted
*1 TBS Molasses
1 tsp. Cinnamon
1 tsp. Vanilla Extract
<u>THREE:</u>
½ Cup Chopped Nuts, *optional*
   Note: Molasses imparts the dark sweetness of brown sugar, which is an important component of standard bread pudding recipes, and adds only a scant amount of carbs to a single serving. You can substitute another sweetener if you prefer.

●Break bread **<u>ONE</u>** into chunky pieces into a buttered baking dish. *Optional: Sprinkle top with **<u>THREE.</u>***
●In mixing bowl with whisk attachment put **<u>TWO</u>** ingredients. Mix on Medium 2 minutes until well blended.
●Pour custard (**<u>TWO</u>**) over bread. Push bread down into the liquid with a fork, going all around, insuring bread is saturated.
●Put dish in unheated oven, turn to 350° F and bake 40-45 minutes, until top is golden and the center springs back when pressed. You can also insert a knife close to the center and if it comes out clean, the pudding is ready.
●Let pudding cool to warm before serving. The flavors will be enhanced. Top with sweetened whipped cream or your favorite low-carb sauce. *So-o good!*

NUTRITION TOTALS:
1 Bun – Calories: 250   Protein: 14 g   Total Carbs: 10 g   Fiber: 5.3 g   NET CARBS: 3 g

Breakfast Buffet Buns

Lightly sweet and buttery, with just the right tender texture for jams and cream cheese, eggs and bacon for breakfast sandwiches – but wonderful by themselves. Can also be baked in a loaf pan. <u>Need: Greased 8-loaf mini-loaf pan or bread pan</u>

<u>ONE:</u>
½ Cup Natural Whey Protein Powder, *unflavored*
½ Cup White Bean Flour
½ Cup Golden Flaxseed Flour, *refined to velvety texture in blender*
½ Cup Almond Flour, *very finely ground*
1 TBS Active Dry Yeast
1 TBS Xanthan Gum
1 tsp. Sea Salt
1 tsp. Diastatic Malt Powder, *optional for gluten-free*
<u>TWO:</u>
4 Egg Whites (½ Cup), *room temperature*
2 Whole Eggs, *room temperature*
¼ Cup Almond Milk, *unsweetened*
9 Drops EZ-Sweetz, *or sweetener equal to 3 TBS*
½ Cup Butter, *soft but not melted*

●Combine **<u>ONE</u>** ingredients in separate bowl, stir well with fork and set aside.

●Put all TWO ingredients in mixing bowl *EXCEPT BUTTER* and mix on Medium 1 minute with paddle attachment until well mixed. With mixer on Low/Stir, add softened butter and increase speed to Medium for 2 minutes to mix in butter.

●Reduce speed to Low/Stir and mix for a full 10 minutes, until batter is elastic.

●Spoon batter into pan/s. If you desire a glossy golden crust, brush with an egg frothed with a bit of salt. Score crisscross design with sharp knife if desired. Set pan in cold oven, turn on oven light and let rise 1 hour. Dough will double in size.

●With pan still in place, turn on oven to 375° F and bake for 20-25 minutes, or until internal temperature is between 190° and 210°. Remove to cooling rack.

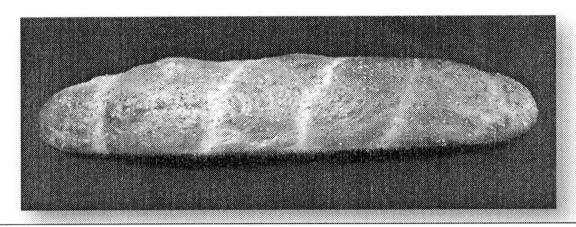

NUTRITION TOTALS:
Entire Loaf – Calories: 1062; Protein: 129 g; Total Carbs: 67 g; Fiber: 19 g; NET CARBS: 48 g
1" Thick Slice: Calories: 66 Protein: 8 g Total Carbs: 4 g Fiber: 1 g NET CARBS: 3 g

Buttermilk French-Style Bread

Great loaf with chewy crust.   Need: Tin foil; French loaf pan; see following pages

ONE:
1 Cup Natural Whey Protein Powder, unflavored
1/2 Cup Almond Flour, *very finely ground* (or Sunflower Flour)
1/4 Cup Buttermilk Powder
1/4 Cup White Bean Flour
2 tsp. Xanthan Gum
1 tsp. Sea Salt
1 tsp. Diastatic Malt Powder (optional)
1 tsp. Baking Powder
TWO:
10 Egg Whites (1 ¼ Cups), *room temperature*
1 TBS Active Dry Yeast
1 TBS Honey
1 tsp Cream of Tartar
THREE:
1 TBS Apple Cider Vinegar

• Prepare the baking pan – see following pages. Spray the foil pan with cooking spray.
•In a separate bowl combine **ONE** ingredients. Blend thoroughly with a whisk and set aside.
•In mixer bowl with whisk attachment put **TWO** ingredients. *Slowly* increase speed to High and whip for 2 minutes into a thick, creamy-white froth.
 •With mixer on Low/Stir add dry ingredients. Remove bowl from stand and stir batter with large spoon, scraping bottom and sides of bowl until *just barely* mixed.
Add vinegar (**THREE**) and quickly stir until *just* blended – *no more.*
•Spoon batter into pan. If it doesn't spread on its own, spread back and forth with back of spoon to ends of pan.
Put pan in cold oven, turn on oven light and let rise 1 hour.
•Remove from oven and with a sharp knife dipped in water, make quick diagonal slices across top a couple inches apart. Top with seeds, if desired. Return pan to oven, turn to 375° F and bake 25-30 minutes, or until internal temperature is about 200°F. Cool before slicing.

Three Options for French Loaf Pans

- **Create a 16" long x 3 ¾" wide x 3 ½" high pan from tin foil:**

  <u>Need: Yard Stick; ball point pen; 12" wide heavy duty foil; baking sheet</u>

Tear a sheet of 12" wide heavy duty foil approximately 24" long.

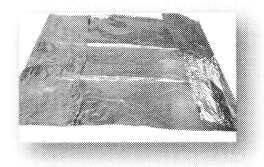

With a gentle touch, mark the foil with a ball point pen 4" inside one of the long edges, one mark on each end. Align the edge of the ruler against the marks and very gently draw a fold line from one mark to the other. From this fold line measure 3 ¾" further in and mark lightly with the pen. Align the edge of the ruler against these marks and draw another fold line. You now have the inside dimensions of the pan. One each of the short ends, measure in 4" from the edge, mark and create fold lines in the same manner.

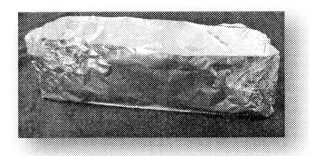

Fold up sides, then fold up ends and wrap excess foil around the sides, squishing it flat. Spray well with cooking spray. **Set pan on baking sheet for support.**

•Use French loaf pan as basic mold:

Need: 16" French loaf pan; 12" wide heavy duty foil.

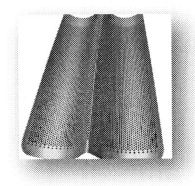 

Line a French loaf pan with a 24" length of foil, centering the foil. Bring up the sides and enclose each end, creating a height of about 3 ½" all around to support and contain the rising dough. Spray with cooking oil.

•Create pan using pre-made foil loaf pans:
Need: Two 8" foil loaf pans;   Baking Sheet

Be very careful using this method. The foil is much heavier and the cut edges can be sharp. Carefully cut off one end of each pan with scissors. Discard ends.

Insert one pan into the other, forming one long pan. Fold over the heavy rim of the top pan to join.   There may be a slight gap on the bottom, as you see in this photo. Press it down as best you can, then line bottom with parchment paper. **Place on baking sheet and spray with cooking oil.**

NUTRITION TOTALS:
Entire Loaf – Calories: 1480; Protein: 105 g; Total Carbs: 88 g; Fiber: 32 g NET CARBS: 56 g
1/12 Serving – Calories: 123; Protein: 8.75 g; Total Carbs: 7 g; Fiber: 2.6 g NET CARBS: 5 g

Challah

Beautiful, golden and delicious   <u>Need: Silicone or metal Challah pan, well-greased</u>

<u>ONE:</u>
½ Cup Natural Whey Protein Powder, *unflavored*
½ Cup White Bean Flour
½ Cup Almond Flour, *very finely ground*
2 TBS Coconut Flour
6 TBS Stevia, *or preferred sweetener*
1 TBS Active Dry Yeast
2 tsp. Xanthan Gum
1 tsp. Diastatic Malt Powder
1 ½ tsp. Sea Salt
1 tsp. Baking Powder
<u>TWO:</u>
6 Egg Whites (3/4 Cup), *room temperature*
1 tsp. Cream of Tartar
<u>THREE:</u>
3 Whole Eggs, *room temperature*
3 TBS. Melted Butter *OR Coconut Oil*
1 TBS Honey
1 TBS Apple Cider Vinegar
½ Cup Warm Water

1 Whole Egg for basting on baked loaf. Optional seeds.

- In separate bowl put **<u>ONE</u>** ingredients. Blend thoroughly with whisk and set aside.
- In small dish put **<u>THREE</u>** ingredients. Mix with fork and set aside.
- In mixer bowl with paddle attachment put **<u>TWO</u>** ingredients. Slowly increase speed to High and mix 1 minute until frothy.
- With mixer on Low/Stir, add liquids. Mix on Medium 1 minute until well blended.
- Turn mixer to Low/Stir and add dry ingredients by spoonsful. Continue mixing on Low/Stir a full 10 minutes to develop elasticity in dough, scraping sides and bottom of bowl if needed.
- Spoon batter into greased Challah pan. Put in cold oven on lowest rack, turn on oven light and let rise for 1 ½ hours.
- Turn oven to 375° F and bake 25-30 minutes, until internal temp reads around 200°. Invert pan onto baking sheet and remove pan from loaf. Brush with beaten whole egg, sprinkle with seeds if desired and return to oven for 5 minutes.

NUTRITION TOTALS:

<u>Entire Loaf</u> – Calories: 1198; Protein: 123g; Total Carbs: 93g; Fiber: 39g; NET CARBS: 46 g

<u>1/12 Serving</u> – Calories: 100; Protein: 10 g; Total Carbs: 8 g; Fiber: 3 g; NET CARBS: 4 g

Chaperone Flat Bread *With option for Moroccan Olive Flat Bread*

Need: Parchment-lined baking sheet. *Tender and delicious. Like all good chaperones, accompanies but does not intrude on a meal.*

One:
½ Cup White Bean Flour
½ Cup Golden Flaxseed Meal
1 Cup Natural Whey Protein Powder, *unflavored*
2 TBS Coconut Flour
1 TBS Active Dry Yeast
2 tsp. Xanthan Gum
1 tsp. Baking Powder
1 tsp. Diastatic Malt Powder
1 tsp. Sea Salt
   For a rich golden color, add 1 tsp. of Tarragon

TWO:
1 ½ cups Warm Water
1 TBS Olive Oil
1 TBS Honey
6 Egg Whites (3/4 Cup)

●In separate bowl combine **ONE** ingredients. Blend thoroughly with whisk and set aside.

●In mixing bowl with paddle attachment put **TWO** ingredients. Beat on Medium for 2 minutes.

●Reduce speed to Low/Stir and add dry ingredients by spoonsful. Mix on Medium for 2 minutes.

●Spoon batter onto middle of a parchment-lined baking sheet. With back of spoon swirl into a circle and outwards until the batter is about 1" thick. *Optional: Sprinkle top with seeds or a spice that will compliment your meal; I like 2 TBS rosemary along with some coarse salt.* Set pan in cold oven, turn on oven light and let rise 1 hour.

●Leaving pan in place, turn oven to 375° F and bake 25-30 minutes, until deep golden brown and internal temperature reads about 200° F.

*Moroccan Olive Option: Put ¼ cup well-drained sliced green olives, with or without pimento, between two paper towels and press out excess moisture. Stir into batter after it has finished mixing until it is evenly mixed throughout. Spoon batter onto middle of parchment-lined pan and swirl out into a circle about 1" thick. Sprinkle top with a combination of: 2 tsp. coarse salt; ½ tsp. garlic powder; ¼ tsp. curry powder; ¼ tsp. paprika; ¼ tsp. cumin. Bake an extra 5 minutes.

Makes Twelve 1" Slices

NUTRITION TOTALS:
1" Slice or 1 Bun:
Calories: 122; Protein: 8 g; Total Carbs: 7 g; Fiber: 3 g; NET CARBS: 4 g

Cinnamon Swirl Bread   *and Buns

O.M.G. Rich delicious pastry.   Need: Greased 12" bread pan.

ONE:
½ Cup Natural Whey Protein Powder, *unflavored*
½ Cup Golden Flaxseed Flour, *refined in blender to velvety texture*
¼ Cup White Bean Flour
¼ Cup Almond Flour, *very finely ground*
2 tsp. Xanthan Gum
2 TBS Coconut Flour
1 tsp. Diastatic Malt Powder, *optional for gluten-free diets*
1 tsp. Sea Salt
1 tsp. Baking Powder
3 TBS Stevia, *or equal preferred sweetener*
   *(if you use liquid, add this to **TWO** ingredients)*

TWO:
1/2 Cup Lukewarm Water
1 TBS Apple Cider Vinegar
1 TBS Honey
1 TBS Active Dry Yeast
1 tsp. Vanilla Extract

THREE:
8 Egg Whites (1 Cup), *room temperature*
1 tsp. Cream of Tartar

Cinnamon Syrup:
3 TBS Melted Butter
9 drops EZ Sweetz *or preferred liquid equal to 3 TBS*
2 tsp. Cinnamon
1 tsp. Cocoa Powder
●Combine in a small bowl and set aside

Frosting:
½ Cup Whipped Cream Cheese
1 TBS EZ-Sweetz or *preferred sweetener*

●In separate bowl combine **ONE** ingredients. Combine with whisk and set aside.
●In small bowl put **TWO** ingredients. Stir until blended and set aside.
●In mixer bowl put **THREE** ingredients, *room temperature*. With whisk attachment slowly turn mixer to High and whip for 5 minutes, or until track drawn with knife-blade doesn't sag.

Cinnamon Swirl Bread – Continued

●Switch from whisk to paddle attachment and turn to Low/Stir. Slowly pour in yeast mixture, then add bowl of dry ingredients by spoonsful. Continue mixing on Low/Stir for 1 minute. Stop mixer, remove bowl and give batter a final few stirs with large spoon.

●Spoon 3-4 spoonsful – about ¼ of the batter - into greased bread pan, spacing them out across bottom. Dribble a couple teaspoons of cinnamon syrup over top of each mound. ***If syrup has thickened, warm in microwave a few seconds for easier drizzling***. Add another 3 spoonsful of batter, filling gaps. Drizzle with a couple teaspoons of syrup. Repeat this process, drizzling last of syrup across top. Put in unheated oven, turn on oven light and let rise 1 hour. Turn on oven to 375° F and bake 25-30 minutes, until top is golden brown and internal temperature is between 190-210° F.

Set pan on rack to cool. Frost the top with sweetened cream cheese. Makes 12 1" thick slices

To Make *Cinnamon Swirl Buns ~

• In a *well-greased* 12-cup muffin pan, put a dollop of batter in bottom of each cup. Drizzle tops with some cinnamon syrup. Repeat process two or three times (depends on spoonsful size), finishing with a drizzle of syrup.
• Put pan in cold oven, turn on oven light and let rise 1 hour.
• Turn oven to 375° F and bake 15-20 minutes, until internal temperature reads between 190° and 210° F.
• Remove pan to cooling rack and let rest a couple minutes, then pop out the buns. They are much easier to remove when the pan is still warm. Frost with sweetened cream cheese when buns are cool.

NUTRITION TOTALS:
1 Muffin – Calories: 81 Protein: 10 g; Total Carbs: 5 g; Fiber: 2 g; NET CARBS: 3 g

English Muffins

Holey English Muffins-with a wonderful hint of buttermilk. <u>Need: 8 greased English muffin rings; electric griddle or two frying pans.</u> *Note: You can also bake these in a 350°F oven, but it is rather like baking pancakes. Frying is the standard way.*

ONE:
½ Cup Natural Whey Protein Powder, *unflavored*
½ Cup Buttermilk Powder
¼ Cup White Bean Flour
¼ Cup Almond Flour, *very finely ground*
2 tsp. Xanthan Gum
1 tsp. gelatin, *unflavored*
1 tsp. Sea Salt
1 tsp. Diastatic Malt Powder (optional)
1 tsp. Baking Powder

TWO:
8 Egg Whites (1 Cup), *room temperature*
½ Cup Warm Water
1 tsp. Cream of Tartar
1 TBS Active Dry Yeast

THREE:
1 TBS Apple Cider Vinegar

●Have a griddle or frying pans holding *well-greased* rings on standby. *Spraying rings with cooking oil works best for me. I have difficulty getting the muffins out of the rings using coconut oil.* If desired, sprinkle about 1 ½ teaspoons (total for all 8 rings) of gluten-free cornmeal into the bottoms and have another 1 ½ teaspoons ready to sprinkle on the tops.

●In a separate bowl combine **ONE** ingredients. Blend thoroughly with a whisk and set aside.

●In mixer bowl with whisk attachment put **TWO** ingredients. *Slowly* increase speed to High and whip for 3 minutes into a cream-colored froth.

English Muffins ~ Continued

●With mixer on Low/Stir add dry ingredients, then remove bowl from stand and stir batter with large spoon, scraping bottom and sides of bowl until *just barely* mixed.

●Add vinegar (**THREE**) and quickly stir until *just* blended – *no more.*

●Put a scant ¼ cup of batter into each ring.

●Hold ring with one hand and with the other hand nudge batter to the edges if it hasn't spread on its own (but it usually does).

●Sprinkle tops with optional gluten-free cornmeal. Let rise 1 hour. They will double in size.
●Turn griddle to 250° F and fry for 8-10 minutes.

NOTE: *Gluten-free "flours" brown very quickly so the temperature needs to be low.* Lift ring with a spatula after a few minutes and if they are browning too much, reduce heat. Tops will start to lose their shine and tackiness when they are ready to turn.

Hint*: Hold a knife against back of the ring for support when you flip the rings over.*

●Fry an additional 5-7 minutes, until internal temperature is about 200° F.

NOTE: If muffins are as brown as you want them but aren't fully cooked, put them on a cookie sheet and bake in a 350° F oven for ten minutes.

These take a little practice but are well worth the effort. Each muffin has 10 grams of protein and with melted butter make a healthful breakfast. They look complicated to make but you will quickly get the knack and learn just the right temperature for your griddle for next time. *Make notes!*

Muffins Before Rise

After 1 Hour Rise

Finished Grilled Muffins

NUTRITION TOTALS:
Entire Loaf - Calories: 1151; Protein: 137 g; Total Carbs: 73 g; Fiber: 24 g; NET CARBS: 50
For standard ½" slice using 12" loaf pan:
Calories: 48; Protein: 6 g; Total Carbs: 3 g; Fiber: 1 g; NET CARBS: 2 g

Fluffy White Bread
Need: Well-greased bread pan

This bread is very similar to the "Light White Sandwich Bread" recipe. It turned out too tender in texture for sandwich making but was such a hit with everyone that I decided to include it for those times when a slice of airy sweet bread with a slather of butter and a cup of hot tea sounds perfect.

ONE:
1 Cup Natural Whey Protein Powder, *unflavored*
¼ Cup White Bean Flour
½ Cup Almond Flour, *very finely ground*
2 TBS Coconut Flour
1 TBS Active Dry Yeast
2 tsp. Xanthan Gum
1 tsp. Sea Salt
1 tsp. Diastatic Malt Powder
1 tsp. Baking Powder

TWO:
½ Cup Warm Water
1 TBS Honey
1 TBS Apple Cider Vinegar
1 tsp. Vanilla Extract
6 Drops EZ-Sweetz, *or preferred sweetener equal to 2 TBS*

THREE:
12 Egg Whites (1 ½ Cups), *room temperature*
1 ½ tsp. Cream of Tartar

- In separate bowl, combine **ONE** ingredients. Mix *thoroughly* with a whisk and set aside.
- In small dish put **TWO** ingredients. Stir to combine and set aside.
- In mixing bowl with whisk attachment, put **THREE ingredients**, room temperature or slightly warmed if you are working in a cold room. Slowly increase speed to High and whip 5 minutes, or until a track drawn through whites with knife doesn't sag.
- Reduce speed to Low/Stir and slowly pour in liquid mixture.
- Add dry ingredients a spoonful at a time until just barely blended. Remove bowl from stand and knock any clinging batter off whisk into bowl. Stir and fold until all dry ingredients are mixed in. Don't over-mix; you don't want to lose the foamy quality.
- Put batter into a greased bread pan and shake back and forth to level dough. Put in cold oven, turn on oven light and let rise 1 hour.
- Leave pan in place and turn on oven to 375° F. Bake 25-30 minutes, or until internal temperature is between 190° and 210° F. Cool on rack before slicing. *Kidding, but try to wait a few minutes.*

NUTRITION TOTALS:
Entire Loaf – Calories: 2046; Protein: 87 g; Total Carbs: 54 g; Fiber: 24 g; NET CARBS: 30 g
1/12 Serving: Calories: 170; Protein: 7 g; Total Carbs: 4.5 g; Fiber: 2 g; NET CARBS: 2.5 g

Focaccia
<u>Need: Baking Sheet</u>
Seriously good – could make a meal of this with a salad.

ONE:
½ Cup Olive Oil
1 TBS Garlic, *finely chopped*
1 TBS Rosemary
1 TBS Basil
1 TBS Oregano
1 tsp. Black Pepper
    Note: These are my favorite spices for focaccia. Use your favorite blend

TWO:
½ Cup Natural Whey Protein Powder, *unflavored*
½ Cup Almond Flour, *very finely ground*
½ Cup Coconut Flour
¼ Cup White Bean Flour
1 TBS Xanthan Gum
1 TBS Stevia, *or preferred sweetener*
1 TBS Active Dry Yeast
1 tsp. Sea Salt
1 tsp. Diastatic Malt Powder, *optional*
1 tsp. Baking Powder

THREE:
8 Egg Whites (1 Cup), *room temperature*
2 TBS Olive Oil
½ Cup Water
1 TBS Apple Cider Vinegar

● In small dish combine **ONE** ingredients, stir and set aside.
● In separate bowl combine **TWO** ingredients, mix with whisk and set aside
● In mixing bowl put **THREE** ingredients. With paddle attachment mix on Low/Medium for 1 minute.
● Reduce speed to Low/Stir and add dry ingredients by spoonsful. Slowly increase speed to Medium and mix for 1 minute. Slowly increase speed to High and whip for 1 minute. Remove bowl from stand.
● Pour 2/3 of oil/spice mixture onto baking sheet and spread to cover bottom of pan.

• Drop dough in 6 evenly spaced mounds onto oil-covered pan.

• Dip fingers into remaining oil in dish and spread out dough, dipping fingers as needed to work the sticky dough. The oil and spices on pan bottom will be caught up in the process; that's fine, just keeping smoothly out the dough. When it is fairly even all around, tap your fingertips firmly into the dough to create dimples all across the top; as the dough rises, spicy oil with gather in them. Dribble on whatever remaining oil you have in dish.

• *Sprinkle top with 1 – 2 tsp. of coarse salt.* Set pan in cold oven, turn on oven light and let rise 1 hour.

• Leaving pan in place, turn on oven to 375° F. Bake 20 minutes, or until top is a rich golden brown.

Numerous focaccia topping recipes can be found online to create exciting, healthful meals.

OLIVE OIL GRADES

Premium Extra Virgin olive oil is the finest quality available—and most expensive. With the lowest acidity, it is best in uncooked dishes where its delicious flavor and aroma can be appreciated.

Extra Virgin is also made from the first pressing of olives with a rich fruity flavor and only slightly more acidity. It is also best used uncooked to be fully enjoyed.

Fine Virgin Oil is a first-press oil with an acidity level of no higher than 1.5%. It is less expensive than extra virgin oil but is close in quality and taste uncooked. Chemicals and high heat are not allowed in the production of extra virgin or **virgin oils.**

Virgin Oil must be less than 2% acidity and cannot contain any refined oil. It is good for cooking but has enough flavor on its own.

Olive Oil and **Pure Olive Oil** are further processed refined blends generally containing 85% refined and 15% virgin or extra virgin to impart a little flavor and aroma. Oils in this grade are used in foods labeled, "packed in olive oil." They withstand heat well and are best used for cooking.

NUTRITION TOTALS: Eight 2" Servings
Entire Loaf – Calories: 870; Protein: 129 g; Total Carbs: 43 g; Fiber: 16 g; NET CARBS: 27 g
Thick 2" Slice – Calories: 109; Protein: 16 g; Total Carbs: 5.3g; Fiber: 2 g; Net Carbs: 3.3 g

French-Style Bread

Need: Tin foil; French loaf pan; see pages 34-35

The crispy crust is golden brown and chewy, with an interior holey texture that springs back when you press it – and bite into it – leaving a wonderful savory aftertaste.

ONE:
1 Cup Natural Whey Protein Powder, *unflavored*
¼ Cup White Bean Flour
¼ Cup Almond Flour, *very finely ground* (or Sunflower Flour)
2 tsp. Xanthan Gum
1 tsp. Sea Salt
1 tsp. Diastatic Malt Powder (optional)
1 tsp. Baking Powder
TWO:
12 Egg Whites (1 ½ Cups), *room temperature*
1 tsp. Cream of Tartar
1 TBS Active Dry Yeast
THREE:
1 TBS Apple Cider Vinegar

●In a separate bowl combine **ONE** ingredients. Blend thoroughly with a whisk and set aside.
●In mixer bowl with whisk attachment put **TWO** ingredients. *Slowly* increase speed to High and whip for 3 minutes. Mixture will look like frothy milk.
●With mixer on Low/Stir add dry ingredients. Remove bowl from stand and stir batter with large spoon, scraping bottom and sides of bowl until *just barely* mixed.
Add vinegar (**THREE**) and quickly stir until *just* blended – *no more*. Pour batter into greased tinfoil pan, put in cold oven, turn on oven light and let rise 1 hour. It will double in size. Remove from oven.
●Preheat oven to 375° F. Slash loaf diagonally with razor a few inches apart and sprinkle top with seeds, if desired. Return loaf to oven and bake 15 minutes at 375° F, then reduce heat to 350° F and bake an additional 10 minutes, until internal temperature is about 200°F.   Try to resist cutting into it for at least 15 minutes. :)

NUTRITION TOTALS:
1 Bun – Calories: 50.5; Protein: 6 g; Total Carbs: 3 g; Fiber: 1 g; NET CARBS: 2 g

Gold Coins

Makes 12 Feather-Light Hors d'oeuvre Mini Buns
<u>Need: Parchment-lined baking sheet</u>

<u>ONE:</u>
½ Cup Natural Whey Protein Powder, *unflavored*
2 TBS Coconut Flour
2 tsp. Xanthan Gum
1 tsp. Active Dry Yeast
1 tsp. Diastatic Malt Powder, *optional for gluten-free diets*
<u>TWO:</u>
3 whole eggs
1 TBS Honey
<u>For sweet pastry, add the following:</u>
1 tsp. Vanilla
3 Drops EZ-Sweetz (or preferred liquid equal to 1 TBS)

<u>THREE:</u>
4 Egg Whites (1/2 Cup), *room temperature*
½ tsp. Cream of Tartar

• In separate bowl put **<u>ONE</u>** ingredients. Blend with a whisk and set aside.
• In separate bowl put **<u>TWO</u>** ingredients. Whip thoroughly with a whisk until frothy and lemon-colored. Remove 1 TBS to small dish and set aside. You will use this to baste the pastry before baking.
• In clean, dry mixer bowl put egg whites, *room temperature*, and cream of tartar. With whisk attachment, slowly increase speed to High and whip 5 minutes into firm, stiff peaks that don't sag.
• Turn mixer to Low/Stir and pour in egg mixture, then add dry ingredients by spoonsful.
• Remove bowl from stand and fold mixture until just blended. Drop by tablespoons onto parchment-lined baking sheet, dividing batter into 12 mounds.
• Baste each mound with reserved yellow egg froth, using the pastry brush to smooth the tops as you baste. Set pan on lower rack in cold oven, turn on oven light and let rise 1 hour. Turn on cold oven to 375° F and bake 15 minutes, or until tops are rich golden brown and internal temp is 195°-210° F. Lift parchment onto rack to cool.
I love these with sweetened cream cheese if I made sweet pastry. For savory appetizers, add a pinch of your favorite spice to compliment the filling – a smidge of dill with a salmon/cream cheese filling. Beautiful to serve.

NUTRITION TOTALS:
Entire Loaf -- Calories: 1712; Protein: 124.5 g; Total Carbs: 103 g; Fiber: 58 g; NET CARBS: 45 g
Serving Size: Two ½" slices from 12" loaf:
    Calories: 143; Protein: 10 g; Total Carbs: 9 g Fiber: 5 g Net Carbs: 4 g

Home-Good Rye Bread   Absolutely Delicious

Need: Greased bread pan ~ *You can also spoon the dough into two baguette pans for thin appetizer slices.*

ONE:
½ Cup Natural Whey Protein Powder, *unflavored*
¼ Cup White Bean Flour
½ Cup Almond Flour
1 Cup Golden Flax Flour, *refined to velvety texture in blender*
1 TBS Active Dry Yeast
1 TBS Stevia or preferred sweetener
1 TBS Caraway Seeds, *whole or ground*
2 tsp. Xanthan Gum
1 tsp. Sea Salt
1 tsp. Baking Powder
1 tsp. Diastatic Malt Powder, *optional*
1 tsp. Deli-Rye Flavor Powder, *or gluten-free rye flavor powder; see page 18*

TWO:
½ Cup Almond Milk
3 TBS Melted Butter (add to Almond Milk to cool down)
2 TBS Coconut Flour
1 TBS Honey

THREE:
8 Egg Whites (1 cup liquid), *room temperature.*
1 tsp. Cream of Tartar

●In separate bowl put **ONE** ingredients. Blend thoroughly with a whisk and set aside.
●In small dish put **TWO** ingredients in this order: melted butter and half of the almond milk, then add coconut flour. Stir to mix. Add remaining almond milk and honey, stir to combine and set aside.
●In mixer bowl put **THREE** ingredients, *room temperature or slightly warmed if working in a cold room.* With whisk attachment slowly increase speed to High and whip for five minutes, until whites are stiff and don't sag when you draw a track with a knife-blade.
●Change from whisk to paddle and turn mixer to Low/Stir. Slowly pour in liquid mixture, then add dry ingredients by spoonsful. Continue mixing on Low for 1 minute. Remove bowl from stand, give batter a few final stirs with large spoon, then spoon into greased bread pan. Put in cold oven, turn on oven light and let rise for 1 hour. Turn oven to 375° F and bake 30-35 minutes (15-20 minutes for baguette pans), or until internal temperature is between 190° and 210° F.

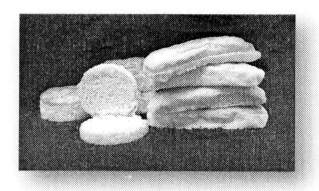

NUTRITION TOTALS:
1 Bun -- Calories: 159; Protein: 12 g; Total Carbs: 9 g; Fiber: 3 g; NET CARBS: 6 g

HOT DOG/HAMBURGER BUNS <u>*Need: 8 greased bun pans</u>
<u>*See Pan Preparation Notes on following pages.</u>

<u>ONE:</u>
1 Cup Natural Whey Protein Powder, *unflavored*
½ Cup Almond Flour, *very finely ground*
¼ Cup White Bean Flour
2 TBS Coconut Flour
2 tsp. Xanthan Gum
1 TBS Stevia, *or sweetener equal to 1 TBS*
1 tsp. Sea Salt
1 tsp. Diastatic Malt Powder, *optional for gluten-free diets*
1 tsp. Baking Powder
<u>TWO:</u>
1 TBS Coconut Oil, *melted*
1 TBS Apple Cider Vinegar
1 TBS Honey
¼ Cup Water
<u>THREE:</u>
12 Egg Whites (1 ½ Cups liquid), *room temperature*
1 tsp. Cream of Tartar
1 TBS Active Dry Yeast

- In separate dish combine <u>**ONE**</u> ingredients. Blend thoroughly with whisk and set aside.
- In small dish put <u>**TWO**</u> ingredients. Stir to blend and set aside.
- Put <u>**THREE**</u> ingredients in mixing bowl, *room temperature*, and with whisk attachment slowly increase speed to High and whip for 1-2 minutes into a good froth—you can't see liquid anymore – *before it starts to form peaks.*
- Reduce speed to Low/Stir and pour in liquids, then add dry ingredients by spoonsful. Remove bowl from stand and finish combining ingredients with a large spoon until just blended.
- Put *just barely* ½ cup of batter into each pan. Dab the dough with your finger to spread to edges of pans. Put pan in oven, turn on oven light and let rise 1 hour.
- Leave pan in place and turn on oven to 375°F. Bake 15 minutes, or until internal temperature is between 190° and 210° F. Mine are usually browned and baked by the time the oven reaches the pre-heat temperature. Remove to rack and let cool before slicing.

Hot Dog/Hamburger Bun Pan Directions

For hamburger buns use English muffin rings, sprayed liberally with cooking spray. For hot dog buns use a foil-lined 4-baguette pan with the foil cut midway in each pan – creating two buns in each pan. Fold up ends of foil to create canoes that will contain the very soft dough as it rises.

If you don't have a baguette pan, you can make molds by folding over (doubling) a square of foil and folding up the sides and ends to create a canoe shape about 2 ½" wide x 7" long x 2 ½" high. Spray each with cooking spray and put on baking sheet for support. A little bit of time and trouble, but it works until the happy day more bread pan choices are available for low-carb gluten-free baking.

This recipe for hamburger buns is a light, fluffy bread with a high rise that may be more bread around your sandwich than you like:

You may prefer Sandwich Slims on page 91

or the Sandwich Bun recipe on page 67.
Both have a denser, chewier texture.

I often divide the dough in half and bake both bun types at the same time.

NUTRITION TOTALS:
Entire Loaf: Calories: 2070; Protein: 139 g; Total Carbs: 108 g; Fiber: 47.6 g NET CARBS: 60.4
1/12 Serving: Calories: 173; Protein: 11.5 g; Total Carbs: 9 g; Fiber: 4 g; NET CARBS: 5 g

Italian Cheese Ring *With Pesto Option*

Need: Lightly greased fluted tube pan or angel-food tube pan sprinkled with sesame seeds.

Elegant to serve, delicious plain or dipped in olive oil sprinkled with herbs

FILLING:

¼ Cup Butter, *very soft*
1 Cup Shredded Mozzarella, *or Italian Cheese Blend*
½ tsp. Italian Seasoning
½ tsp. Garlic Powder

ONE:

½ Cup Natural Whey Protein Powder, *unflavored*
½ Cup Golden Flaxseed Meal
½ Cup White Bean Flour
½ Cup Almond Flour
2 TBS Coconut Flour
1 TBS Active Dry Yeast
3 TBS Stevia, *or preferred sweetener equal*
2 tsp. Xanthan Gum
1 tsp. Sea Salt
1 tsp. Diastatic Malt Powder
1 tsp. Baking Powder

TWO:

½ Cup Warm Water
2 Whole Eggs
1 TBS Honey
1 TBS Apple Cider Vinegar

THREE:

6 Egg Whites, *room temperature*
½ tsp. Cream of Tartar

- In separate bowl put **FILLING** ingredients. Blend well with fork and set aside.
- In large separate bowl put **ONE** ingredients. Blend thoroughly with whisk and set aside.
- In separate bowl put **TWO** ingredients. Blend well with fork (*eggs do not have to be completely broken down*) and set aside.
- In mixing bowl with whisk attachment put **THREE** ingredients. Slowly increase speed to High and whip for 2 minutes into a good thick froth (you can't see any liquid).
- Reduce speed to Low/Stir and pour in liquid **TWO** ingredients. Add dry **ONE** ingredients by spoonsful. Increase speed to Medium and mix for 2 minutes.
- Spoon half of batter into pan, swirling it around the tube with back of spoon to level. (*I hold the spoon in place with one hand and with the other, turn the pan round and round to spread evenly.*) Add **FILLING** mixture by small spoonsful around the center tube and slightly outward to within 1" of sides of pan. Spoon remaining batter evenly over filling, then spread outward to connect top batter with lower layer of batter (easy and fast with the hand/pan-turning method).
- Put pan in cold oven, turn on oven light and let rise 1 hour. Turn oven to 375° F and bake 25-30 minutes, until internal temperature is between 190° and 210° F. You will see the butter bubbling up around the center tube. Invert immediately and serve warm. The edges have a delicious golden crunch; the savory melted cheese and bread is yum. Enjoy!

   For a great variation, replace the butter and spices in the filling with ¼ Cup pesto combined with the 1 Cup of cheese.

NUTRITION TOTALS:
1 Bun: Calories 114; Protein: 11 g; Total Carbs: 9 g; Fiber: 4 g; NET CARBS: 5 g

Light and Chewy Dinner Rolls *or* Sandwich Buns

Slightly dense yet light and chewy.
Need: For Dinner Rolls - Greased (even if it is non-stick) mini-loaf pan.
For Buns – 8 greased English muffins rings; parchment-lined baking sheet

ONE:
½ Cup Natural Whey Protein Powder, *unflavored*
½ Cup Golden Flaxseed Flour, *refined to velvety texture in blender*
¼ Cup White Bean Flour
¼ Cup Almond Flour, *very finely ground*
1 TBS Stevia, *or preferred sweetener*
2 tsp. Xanthan Gum
1 tsp. Diastatic Malt Powder
1 tsp. Sea Salt
1 tsp. Baking Powder

TWO:
8 Egg Whites (1 Cup), *room temperature*
1 TBS Active Dry Yeast
1 TBS Apple Cider Vinegar
1 TBS Honey

●In separate bowl combine **ONE** ingredients. Mix thoroughly with a whisk and set aside.
●In mixer bowl with paddle attachment put **TWO** ingredients. Gradually increase speed to High and whip for 2 minutes into a thickening beige froth.
●Turn speed to Low/Stir and add dry ingredients by spoonsful. Increase speed to Medium-High and mix 2 minutes into a smooth batter.
●For Dinner Rolls: Spoon batter into 8 greased mini-loaf pans. Dip fingers into a small dish of cool water and smooth tops and sides of rolls until they are smooth and glossy (it takes very little water to achieve this.) Set pan in cold oven, turn on oven light and let rise for 1 hour. Turn oven to 375 ° F and bake 20 minutes, until internal temp is between 190° – 210° F. *Optional: Baste tops with butter.*
●For Sandwich Buns: Spoon batter into 8 well-greased English muffin rings resting on a parchment-lined baking sheet. Hold a ring with one hand and with the other hand dip fingertips into cool water and dab the dough to ring edges. When finished, quickly lift away ring molds so the dough can spread as it rises. Put pan in cold oven, turn on oven light and let rise 1 hour. Turn oven to 375° F and bake 20 minutes, or until internal temp is between 190° – 210° F. *Optional: Baste tops with butter.*

NUTRITION TOTALS:
1 of 8 Rolls: Calories: 98.6; Protein: 4 g; Total Carbs: 10 g; Fiber: 4 g; NET CARBS: 6 g

Lightly Lemon Rolls
Need: Parchment-lined baking sheet

With just a hint of lemon this is a wonderful dinner or brunch roll, especially served with seafood. I left these out overnight – uncovered – and the next day they were still soft and delicious, with a slightly chewy crust.

ONE:
½ Cup Natural Whey Protein Powder, *unflavored*
½ Cup Coconut Flour
¼ Cup White Bean Flour
2 tsp. Xanthan Gum
1 TBS Active Dry Yeast
1 tsp. Sea Salt
1 tsp. Diastatic Malt Powder, *optional*
1 tsp. Baking Powder
TWO:
½ Cup Almond Milk, *unsweetened*
2 TBS Lemon Juice
1 TBS Coconut Oil
2 tsp. Honey
Liquid sweetener equal to 3 TBS
6 Egg Whites (3/4 Cup), *room temperature*
THREE:
1 TBS butter, melted
1 tsp. Honey

- In separate bowl put **ONE** ingredients. Combine with a whisk and set aside
- In mixing bowl put **TWO** ingredients in this order: Almond milk, then lemon juice. Stir to blend and let sit a minute to interact. Add oil, honey (*honey rolls right out of the measuring spoon when you add oil first*), and egg whites. With paddle beater slowly increase speed to Medium and mix 1 minute.
- Decrease speed to Low/Stir and add dry ingredients by spoonsful. Increase speed to Medium for 1 minute, then increase speed to High for 1 minute, whipping the batter fine and smooth.
- Spoon batter onto parchment lined baking sheet into 6 or eight mounds, depending on how large you want the rolls. Put in cold oven, turn on oven light and let rise 1 hour.
- Turn oven on to 375° F and bake 20 minutes or until internal temp is between 190° and 210° F. Remove to cooling rack and brush tops with combined **THREE** ingredients while rolls are still warm.

NUTRITION TOTALS: **Two** ½" thick slices from 9" loaf
Calories: 124; Protein: 14 g; Total Carbs: 8 g; Fiber: 2.6 g; NET CARBS: 5.4 g

Light White Sandwich Bread

White bread without the guilt! This nutritious bread is very similar to the "Fluffy White Bread Recipe" but is not as sweet and has a better body for peanut butter, mayonnaise, etc. <u>Need: 9" x 5" greased loaf pan.</u> *Note: You can also use an 8" pan for a higher loaf, but put it on a baking sheet. If the egg whites have whipped especially high (room temperature, altitude and other elements can affect this) some of the dough may spill over the pan while baking.*

ONE:
1 Cup Natural Whey Protein Powder, *unflavored*
¼ Cup White Bean Flour
½ Cup Almond Flour, *very finely ground*
2 TBS Coconut Flour
1 TBS Active Dry Yeast
2 tsp. Xanthan Gum
1 tsp. Sea Salt
1 tsp. Diastatic Malt Powder
1 tsp. Baking Powder

TWO:
½ Cup Warm Water
1 TBS Honey
1 TBS Apple Cider Vinegar
1 tsp. Vanilla Extract
*3 Drops EZ-Sweetz, *or preferred sweetener*

THREE:
10 Egg Whites (1 ¼ Cups) room temperature
 1 tsp. Cream of Tartar

- In separate bowl combine **ONE** ingredients. Mix *thoroughly* with a whisk. Set aside.
- In small dish put **TWO** ingredients. Stir to combine and set aside.
- In mixing bowl free of any trace of grease, put **THREE ingredients**, room temperature – or slightly warmer if you are working in a cold room. (Set container of whites in a bowl of hot tap-water for a few minutes). With whisk attachment slowly increase speed to High and whip 5 minutes, or until a track drawn through whites with knife doesn't sag.
- Reduce speed to Low/Stir and slowly pour in liquid mixture.
- Add dry ingredients a spoonful at a time until just barely blended. Remove bowl from stand and knock any clinging batter off whisk into bowl. Stir and fold until all dry ingredients are mixed in. Don't over-mix; you don't want to lose the foamy quality.
- Put batter into a greased (even if it is nonstick) bread pan and shake back and forth to level dough. Put in cold oven, turn on oven light and let rise 1 hour.
- Leave pan in place and turn on oven to 375˚ F. Bake 30 minutes, or until internal temperature is between 190˚ and 210˚ F.

NUTRITION TOTALS: 1 muffin or 1/8 portion:
Calories: 185: Protein: 13 g; Total Carbs: 8 g; Fiber: 4 g; NET CARBS: 4 g

Nut & Seed Bread

Absolutely fabulous – a family favorite!

<u>Need: Greased 8" round cake pan or 8-cup muffin pan, well-greased</u>

ONE:

8 Egg Whites (3/4 Cup), *room temperature*
½ Cup Almond Milk, *unsweetened*
1 Whole Egg
1 TBS Olive Oil
1 TBS Molasses
3 Drops EZ-Sweetz, *or preferred liquid sweetener equal to 1 TBS*

TWO:

½ Cup Golden Flaxseed Flour, *refined to velvety texture in blender*
½ Cup Almond Flour
½ Cup Vanilla Whey Protein Powder
¼ Cup Sunflower Flour (*If you can't find "sunflour," *grind raw sunflower kernels to velvety texture in blender. You can also substitute almond flour but flavor won't be as rich.*)
2 TBS Coconut Flour
1 TBS Active Dry Yeast
1 TBS Poppy or Chia Seeds
1 TBS Sesame Seeds
1 tsp. Sea Salt
1 tsp. Diastatic Malt Power, *optional for gluten-free*
1 tsp. Baking Powder

Grind only ½ cup at a time for 30 seconds or flour will overheat and clump.

• Put **ONE** ingredients in mixing bowl and let come to room temperature while you prepare dry ingredients. Don't mix yet.

• In separate bowl combine **TWO** ingredients. Blend well by hand with a whisk and set aside.

• With mixer whisk attachment, mix **ONE** ingredients for 2 minutes, *slowly* increasing speed to Medium/High until mixture is a golden froth.

●Reduce speed to Low/Stir and add dry ingredients by spoonsful. Increase speed to Medium and mix for 2 minutes. Batter will be somewhat thin and cake-like.

●Pour batter into greased 8" cake pan and sprinkle top with sesame, poppy or chia seeds, or a combination.   Or, put about ¼ cup of batter into 8 muffin pans and sprinkle with chia seeds. Set in cold oven, turn on oven light and let rise 1 hour.

●Turn over to 375°F and bake for 25-30 minutes (15-20 minutes for muffin pan). If you look while it is baking you will see an interesting bubbling action in the dough, creating a wonderful airy texture. When internal temperature is between 190° and 210° F, move to cooling rack. Remove from pan while still warm and enjoy, slathered with butter.

Chia Seed has been called the "it" food of 2013 — the year it officially outgrew its "chi-chi-chi chia" fuzzy pottery status. The nutty tasting whole grain seeds are either white or black and provide a tremendous source of nutrients.

Chia is a member of the mint family. It absorbs up to 12 times its own weight, expanding to curb our appetite, and contains the highest antioxidant activity of any whole food.

Unlike flaxseed, chia seeds can be stored for long periods without becoming rancid and don't require grinding to reap the health benefits.

Chia seeds contain 10 grams of fiber in only 2 tablespoons.

The outer layer of chia seeds swell when mixed with liquids to form a gel, which can be used as an egg replacement in recipes calling for one or two whole eggs. For 1 egg mix 1 TBS of seed with 3 TBS water and let rest for 15 minutes.

Researchers suggest this same gel-forming process takes place in the stomach, creating a barrier between carbohydrates and the enzymes that break them down, thus slowing the conversion into sugar.

Insects hate the chia plant, so it's easy to find organic seeds.

It is said that 1 tablespoon of Chia can sustain a person for 24 hours.

NUTRITION TOTALS:
Whole Loaf: Calories: 1430; Protein: 87 g; Total Carbs: 64.3; Fiber: 44.3 g; NET CARBS: 20 g
1/8 Serving: Calories: 179; Protein: 11 g; Total Carbs: 8 g; Fiber: 5.5 g; NET CARBS: 2.5 g

Onion Dill Casserole Bread

<u>Need: 1 ½ - 2 qt. liberally greased casserole dish or 12" bread pan</u>

This is a delicious, moist bread anytime, but especially so served with fish or seafood.

ONE:

1 Cup Golden Flaxseed Meal, *refined to velvety texture in blender*

½ Cup Almond Flour, *very finely ground*

¼ Cup Natural Whey Protein Powder, *unflavored*

2 TBS Coconut Flour

2 TBS Stevia, *or equivalent sweetener*

1 TBS Instant Chopped Onion

1 TBS Active Dry Yeast

2 tsp. Dill Seed

2 tsp Xanthan Gum

1 tsp. Sea Salt

1 tsp. Baking Powder

1 tsp. Diastatic Malt Powder, *optional*

TWO:

½ Cup Sour Cream, *regular*	1 TBS Butter
1 Whole Egg	1 TBS Honey

THREE:

6 Egg Whites (3/4 Cup) *room temperature*

1 tsp. Cream of Tartar

●In separate bowl combine ingredients in **ONE**. Blend well with whisk and set aside.

●In small, microwave-safe bowl combine **TWO** ingredients in this order: Put sour cream and butter in microwave less than 1 minute, until just warm and butter is melting. Blend together and add the egg, combining the three with a fork into a warm, creamy blend of soft yellow.

●Put **THREE** ingredients, room temperature, in mixing bowl and with whisk attachment whip on High for 5 minutes, until knife track drawn through whites doesn't sag.

● Change beaters from whisk to paddle. On Low/Stir slowly add liquid mixture, then add dry ingredients by spoonsful until just blended. Remove bowl from stand and stir batter with large spoon until ingredients are combined.

●*Be sure that the pan or bowl is greased liberally. If it isn't you will have a chore removing the loaf. (I learned this the hard way).* Spoon in the batter, set in cold oven, turn on oven light and let rise 1 hour.

●Turn oven to 375° F and bake 30 minutes, or until internal temperature is between 190° and 210° F.

●Remove loaf from pan to cool on wire rack. While still warm, brush top with butter and sprinkle with coarse salt.

NUTRITION TOTALS:
Whole Pizza – Calories: 1110; Protein: 94 g; Total Carbs: 80 g; Fiber: 37 g; NET CARBS: 43
1/4 Serving - Calories: 277.5; Protein: 23.5 g; Total Carbs: 20 g; Fiber: 9 g; NET CARBS: 11

Pizza Dough

<u>Need: 16" greased pizza pan; tin foil.</u>

This makes a nice yeasty raised crust with crisp edges. It lacks the "pull" of standard pizza crusts but has enough support to be held in hand even with multiple toppings. A generous ¼ serving of this 16" crust has 277 calories, 23 g protein, 11 net carbs and 9 g of fiber, more than enough to satisfy the hungriest pizza craving.

ONE:

½ Cup Golden Flaxseed Meal, *refined to a velvety texture in blender*
½ Cup Natural Whey Protein Powder, *unflavored*
¼ Cup Buttermilk Powder
¼ Cup White Bean Flour
¼ Cup Almond Flour, *very finely ground*
2 TBS Coconut Flour
1 TBS Active Dry Yeast
2 tsp. Xanthan Gum
1 tsp. Sea Salt
1 tsp. Diastatic Malt Powder, *optional for gluten-free diets*
1 tsp. White Cheddar Seasoning, *optional but tasty; found on grocery popcorn seasoning shelf*

TWO:

8 Egg Whites (1 Cup), *room temperature*
1 TBS Apple Cider Vinegar
2 TBS Olive Oil
1 TBS Honey
½ Cup Warm Water

●In separate bowl combine **ONE** ingredients. Blend well with a whisk and set aside.

●In mixing bowl with paddle attachment put **TWO** ingredients. Slowly increase speed to Medium/High and whip 2 minutes into a thick froth.

Pizza Dough – Continued

●Reduce speed to Low/Stir and add dry ingredients by spoonsful. Continue mixing on Low/Stir a full 10 minutes to develop elastic quality.

●Spoon batter into center of pizza pan and with back of spoon spread and swirl the dough outward while turning pan with other hand. Even out to a fairly consistent thickness.

● Set pan in cold oven, turn on oven light and let rise 1 hour.

●Tear a large piece of foil – enough to amply cover top of pan – and fold it in half to create a tent crease. Attach the foil on two sides of the pan, leaving the peaked areas of the foil tent open to allow steam to escape. This protects the top from overbrowning during the first phase bake.

● Put tented pan in oven and turn on to 375° F. Bake for 12 minutes. During this time prepare your toppings.

● Remove from oven and set aside foil tent to wrap any leftovers. *Quickly add toppings* and return to oven to bake 15-20 minutes. By allowing the crust to partially bake, the toppings will not soak into the soft dough.

● The bottom of the crust will likely be dark brown but this does not affect the flavor.

NOTE: The baked dough shell freezes well for later use. Just seal it with foil.

The protein in ¼ serving of the crust alone is equivalent to 4 whole eggs, and as much fiber as ¾ cup of sunflower seeds. Not only pizza without the guilt, but great for us!

NUTRITION TOTALS:
Whole Loaf -- Calories: 888; Protein: 110 g; Total Carbs: 65 g; Fiber: 21 g; NET CARBS: 44 g
1/8 Serving -- Calories: 111; Protein: 14 g; Total Carbs: 8 g; Fiber: 2.6 g; NET CARBS: 5.4 g

Pull-Apart Pastry

Melt in your mouth delicious   <u>Need: Parchment-covered baking sheet</u>

<u>ONE:</u>
1 Cup Natural Whey Protein Powder, *unflavored*
¼ Cup White Bean Flour
¼ Cup Almond Flour, *very finely ground*
2 TBS Coconut Flour
2 tsp. Xanthan Gum
1 tsp. Diastatic Malt Powder, *optional for gluten-free diets*
1 tsp. Sea Salt
1 tsp. Baking Powder
3 TBS Stevia, *or preferred sweetener equal to 3 TBS*
    (if you use liquid, add this to TWO ingredients)

TWO:
1 Cup Warm Water
1 tsp. Vanilla Extract
1 TBS Honey
1 TBS Active Dry Yeast

THREE:
6 Egg Whites (3/4 Cup), *room temperature*
1 tsp. Cream of Tartar

●In separate bowl combine **<u>ONE</u>** ingredients. Blend thoroughly with whisk and set aside.

●In small dish put **TWO** ingredients. Stir until blended and set aside.

●In mixer bowl with whisk attachment put **<u>THREE</u>** ingredients. Slowly turn mixer to High and whip for 5 minutes, until track drawn with knife-blade doesn't sag.

●Switch from whisk to paddle attachment and turn to Low/Stir. Slowly pour in yeast mixture, then add dry ingredients by spoonsful. Continue mixing on Low/Stir for 1 minute.

●Stop mixer, remove bowl and give batter a final few stirs with large spoon.

●Spoon batter onto parchment-lined large baking sheet, forming a mound the size of a dinner plate. Put in unheated oven, turn on oven light and let rise 1 hour.

●Turn on oven to 375°F and bake 25 minutes, until top is golden brown and internal temperature is between 190°-210° F

●Set pan on rack to cool. The baked pastry will collapse into a delectable texture. When cool, lightly frost with sweetened cream cheese (lemon-flavored in wonderful), or sprinkle with cinnamon and top with whipped cream. The possibilities are endless with this heavenly pastry. Servings can either be torn off or cut into long slices.

NUTRITION TOTALS:
Whole Loaf: Calories: 1711; Protein: 101 g; Total Carbs: 71 g; Fiber: 40 g; NET CARBS: 31 g
1/12 Serving: Calories: 143; Protein: 8 g; Total Carbs: 6 g; Fiber: 3 g; NET CARBS: 3 g

Pumpernickel Bread
A dense, dark, delicious, aromatic loaf
<u>Need: 2 qt. greased oven-safe bowl, *or 12" bread pan or baguette pans*</u>
Note: If you love pumpernickel and rye bread, it is worth the small investment for one of the rye-flavor powders, which will make many, many loaves.

<u>ONE:</u>
½ Cup Natural Whey Protein Powder, *unflavored*

¼ Cup White Bean Flour

½ Cup Almond Flour

½ Cup Golden Flaxseed Meal, *refined to velvety texture in blender*

2 tsp. Xanthan Gum

3 TBS Cocoa Powder

1 tsp. Sea Salt

1 tsp. Baking Powder

1 tsp. Diastatic Malt Powder, *optional for gluten-free*

1 tsp. Deli-Rye Flavor Powder, *or gluten-free rye flavor powder; see page 18*

2-3 tsp. Caraway Seeds, *optional*

1 tsp. Fennel Seeds, *optional*

<u>TWO:</u>
8 Egg Whites (1 Cup), *room temperature*

1 TBS Active Dry Yeast

3 TBS Coconut Oil, *room temperature* (or Olive Oil)

1 TBS Apple Cider Vinegar

9 Drops EZ Sweetz, *or liquid sweetener equal to 3 TBS*

1 tsp. Coffee Extract (*or 1 TBS instant coffee*)

• In separate bowl put **<u>ONE</u>** ingredients. Blend thoroughly with a whisk and set aside.

• In mixer bowl put **<u>TWO</u>** ingredients. With paddle attachment slowly increase speed to Medium and mix for two minutes.

• With mixer on Low/Stir, add dry ingredients by spoonsful, then mix on Medium 3 minutes. Batter will be like thick chocolate cake batter. Spoon into greased bowl*, put in cold oven, turn on oven light and let rise for 1 hour. Turn oven to 375° F and bake 30-35 minutes, or until internal temperature is between 190° and 210° F.

I like to make a foil mold of a spiral imprint used for stamping conventional bread loaves. Just press heavy-duty foil onto the mold, pinching foil tightly to conform to the design. Spray with cooking oil, put in bottom of bowl, imprint-side-up so it will press into the dough, then put dough on top. Any cookie cutter design will also work. It adds an interesting and impressive feature to the finished loaf.

Nutrition Totals:

Whole Batch: Calories: 784; Protein: 117 g; Total Carbs: 60 g; Fiber: 18 g; NET CARBS: 42 g
1 of 12: Calories: 65; Protein: 10 g; Total Carbs: 5 g; Fiber: 1.5 g; NET CARBS: 3.5 g

Raised Glazed Doughnuts

So good, especially just out of the fryer and glazed.

NEED: Parchment lined baking sheet; deep fryer with recommended level of oil; pair of tongs; two large spoons; paper towels

ONE:
1 Cup Natural Whey Protein Powder, *unflavored*
¼ White Bean Flour
2 TBS Coconut Flour
1 TBS Active Dry Yeast
2 tsp. Xanthan Gum
1 tsp. Sea Salt
1 tsp. Diastatic Malt Powder, optional for gluten-free diets
1 tsp. Baking Powder

TWO:
1 TBS Honey
¼ Cup Water
2 TBS Butter
9 Drops EZ-Sweetz, *or liquid sweetener equal to 3 TBS (If you use a powdered sweetener, add to **ONE** ingredients)*

THREE:
8 Egg Whites (1 Cup liquid), room temperature
1 tsp. Cream of Tartar

GLAZE:
¼ Cup Almond Milk, *unsweetened*
1 Egg White
1 tsp. Butter Flavor
4 TBS Stevia *or preferred powdered sweetener*

- Put almond milk and egg white in small dish, stir until combined and microwave 30 seconds.
- Stop and stir, then microwave another 30 seconds. Repeat process one more time to insure egg white is cooked and evenly mixed with almond milk.
- Add sweetener and flavoring, stir to blend and set aside.

- In separate bowl combine **ONE** ingredients, mix thoroughly with a whisk and set aside.
- In small dish stir **TWO** ingredients. Microwave until butter is mostly melted, stir again and set aside.

•Put **THREE** ingredients, *room temperature*, in mixing bowl with whisk attachment and whip on High for 5 minutes until whites are high, glossy and stiff.

•Reduce speed to Low/Stir and pour in liquid **TWO** ingredients, then add dry **ONE** ingredients by spoonsful. As soon as they are added, remove bowl from stand and mix with large spoon until all ingredients are *just* mixed in. Batter will be beautiful, light and foamy.

~ ~ ~

●There are three ways to prepare the dough for frying:

Option One is the easiest and to me the tastiest method. Spoon the dough into a large bowl, put in a cold oven, turn on oven light and let rise for 1 hour.

•Make **GLAZE** and set aside.

•Heat oil to 350° F.

•Holding two large spoons, one in each hand, dip them into the hot oil, scoop out a spoonful of dough and slide it into the oil with the other spoon. Dip spoons again and repeat. You will only have time to do 4 or 5 as they brown quickly. Turn with tongs and when they are a rich dark brown and crunchy, about 1 minute, remove with tongs to paper towels. Brush with Glaze on both sides when all are fried.

Option Two: The dough is so soft it needs support while it is rising and while lifting into the hot oil. After batter is mixed, drop by spoonsful into 9 or 12 evenly spaced mounds on parchment paper.

●Cut parchment paper with scissors between the mounds both ways so that each doughnut is sitting in the middle of its own square of parchment paper. *See illustration.* This step makes the frying process much easier.

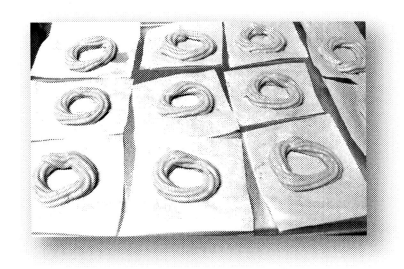

●Set pan in cold oven, turn on oven light and let rise for 1 hour. This is good time to make the **Glaze** and have it standing by. Heat oil to 350˚ F.

●Lift up a square of parchment holding doughnut and insert into hot oil until 4 or 5 are added. As soon as the doughnut edges turn light brown, with the tongs grab hold of a corner of the paper and turn the doughnut over. The paper will peel right off with the tongs to be set aside. Let doughnuts fry about 20 seconds, then turn them over and let fry a few more seconds before lifting them out with tongs onto paper towels. Repeat process; it only takes a minute for doughnuts to reach rich brown stage. Brush with Glaze on both sides when all are fried. *Wonderful filled with whipped cream.*

Option Three: After batter is mixed, put into a pastry bag and make doughnut circles on parchment paper. If tip isn't wide enough to create an average-sized doughnut the first time around, go around again until it's the size you want. Evenly space each one so that each will be sitting on its own parchment square when you cut between them.

●Follow cutting, rise time and frying instructions in **Option Two.**

NUTRITION TOTALS:
1 Bun: Calories: 114; Protein: 11 g; Total Carbs: 8 g; Fiber: 3 g; NET CARBS: 5 g

Sandwich Slims   Perfect round thin buns
<u>Need: Parchment covered baking sheet; 8 greased English muffin rings</u>

ONE:
½ Cup Natural Whey Protein, *unflavored*
½ Cup Golden Flaxseed Meal, *refined to velvety texture in blender*
¼ Cup White Bean Flour
¼ Cup Almond Flour, *or sunflour or hemp flour*
1 TBS Stevia *or preferred sweetener*
1 TBS Active Dry Yeast
2 tsp. Xanthan Gum
1 tsp. Sea Salt
1 tsp. Baking Powder
1 tsp. Diastatic Malt Powder, *optional*
<u>TWO:</u>
8 Egg Whites (1 Cup), *room temperature*
½ Cup Warm Water
1 TBS Honey

● Have greased rings standing by on parchment-covered baking sheet.
● In separate bowl combine **<u>ONE</u>** ingredients. Blend thoroughly with whisk and set aside.
● In mixing bowl with whisk attachment, put **<u>TWO</u>** ingredients. Slowly increase speed to High and whip for ½ - 2 minutes into a good froth (*you can't see liquid anymore but before peaks start to form*).
● With mixer on Low/Stir add dry ingredients by spoonsful until just blended.
● Remove bowl from stand and give batter a few more stirs with large spoon to finish combining dry ingredients. Put ¼ cup batter into each ring, going around again dividing up remaining batter with spoon. Hold a ring with one hand and with the other dab batter to edge of ring. As soon as you have finished all eight, quickly lift and remove the rings, allowing batter to spread into perfect rounds. Sprinkle tops with seeds, if desired. Put pan in cold oven, turn on oven light and let rise 1 hour.
● Turn oven to 375° F and bake 20 minutes or until internal temperature is between 190° and 210° F. Transfer to rack to cool.

NUTRITION TOTALS:
Whole Loaf – Calories: 1220; Protein: 95 g; Total Carbs: 92 g; Fiber: 34 g. NET CARBS: 58 g
1/8 Serving – Calories: 152.5; Protein: 12 g; Total Carbs: 11.5 g; Fiber: 4.3 g; NET CARBS: 7.2 g

Sesame Loaf
If you like the flavor of sesame seeds, you will love this savory loaf.
<u>Need: Greased French loaf pan</u>

One:
½ Cup White Bean Flour

½ Cup Natural Whey Protein Powder, *unflavored*

½ Cup Sesame Seed "Flour," *as fine as you can grind whole raw sesame seeds*

2 TBS Coconut Flour

2 tsp. Xanthan Gum

1 tsp. Sea Salt

1 tsp. Diastatic Malt Powder, *optional for gluten-free diets*

1 tsp. Baking Powder

TWO:
8 Egg Whites (1 Cup), *room temperature*

1 TBS Sesame Seed Oil

1 TBS Honey

1 TBS Apple Cider Vinegar

1 TBS Active Dry Yeast

½ Cup Warm Water

Raw sesame seeds to sprinkle on loaf.

●In separate bowl combine **ONE** ingredients. Blend thoroughly with whisk. You may have tiny lumps of ground sesame seed and that's okay. Set aside.

●In mixing bowl with whisk attachment put **TWO** ingredients. Mix on Medium for 2 minutes until frothy.

●Reduce speed to Low/Stir and add dry ingredients by spoonsful. Increase speed to Medium and mix for one minute.

●Spoon batter into an oblong shape in a French loaf pan. Spread and level batter with fingertips into a loaf about 12-14" long. Sprinkle top liberally with sesame seeds, set loaf in cold oven, turn on oven light and let rise 1 hour.

●Leaving pan in place, turn oven on to 375° F and bake 25 minutes, until nicely browned and internal temperature is between 190° and 210°F.

NUTRITION TOTALS:
1 Biscuit: Calories: 132.5; Protein: 3 g; Total Carbs: 4 g; Fiber: 2.55 g; NET CARBS: 1.5 g

Supreme Yeast Drop Biscuits

Need: <u>Parchment lined baking sheet</u>

This recipe is a little more complicated but easy to do and well worth the extra effort.

<u>ONE:</u>
½ Cup Coconut Flour
½ Cup Almond Flour
2 tsp Xanthan Gum
1 tsp. Diastatic Malt Powder
<u>TWO</u>:
1 Cup Water
½ Cup Butter
1 tsp. Sea Salt
<u>THREE:</u>
1 TBS Active Dry Yeast
1 tsp. Baking Powder
<u>FOUR</u>:
3 Whole Eggs, room temperature
<u>FIVE:</u>
1 TBS Apple Cider Vinegar

- In separate bowl combine put **<u>ONE</u>** ingredients. Mix with whisk and set aside.
- In medium saucepan put **<u>TWO</u>** ingredients. Bring to boil and when butter has melted, remove pan from heat.
- Add **<u>ONE</u>** ingredients and stir. It will combine quickly.
- Put fragrant dough into mixing bowl, turn to Low/Stir and let mix a couple minutes to cool down.
- In the meantime, combine **<u>THREE</u>** ingredients in a small dish. Stir to blend and set aside.
- With mixer off, add whole eggs to dough one at a time, breaking yolks with a knife or fork. Slowly turn mixer to Medium and mix for 2 minutes, until eggs are thoroughly blended.
- Reduce speed to Low/Stir and add the yeast/baking powder. Mix on Medium 1 minute.
- Remove bowl from stand. Have a large serving spoon on hand. Add vinegar and stir until just combined.
- Drop dough into 12 egg-sized mounds on parchment paper, put in cold oven, turn on oven light and let rise 1 hour. There is a little rise, not a lot, but the texture changes.
- Turn oven to 375° F and bake 20 minutes, or until internal temperature reads close to 200° F.

NUTRITION TOTALS: Serving Size: Two ½" Slices
Whole Loaf -- Calories: 1370; Protein: 90 g; Total Carbs: 58.6 g; Fiber: 34.6 g; NET CARBS: 24 g
Per Serving: Calories: 152; Protein: 10 g; Total Carbs: 6.5 g; Fiber: 4 g; NET CARBS: 2.6 g

Whole Goodness Sandwich Bread

<u>Need: Greased 9" x 5" bread pan</u>

A delicious sandwich bread, wonderful eaten just plain.

ONE:
½ Cup Golden Flaxseed Flour, *refined to velvety texture in blender*
½ Cup Almond Flour (or substitute Sunflower Flour)
¼ Cup Natural Whey Protein Powder, *unflavored*
¼ Cup Buttermilk Powder
¼ Cup White Bean Flour
2 TBS Coconut Flour
1 TBS Active Dry Yeast
2 tsp. Xanthan Gum
1 ½ tsp. Sea Salt
1 tsp. Diastatic Malt Powder
1 tsp. Baking Powder

TWO:
½ Cup Water, *lukewarm*
3 TBS Coconut Oil, melted
1 TBS Apple Cider Vinegar
1 TBS Honey
1 tsp. Vanilla Extract
6 Drops EZ-Sweetz, *or preferred liquid sweetener equal to 2 TBS*

THREE:
8 Egg Whites (1 Cup), *room temperature*
1 tsp. Cream of Tartar

●In separate bowl combine **ONE** ingredients. Mix thoroughly with a whisk and set aside. *Take a moment to smell the flours – this is such a fragrant healthful blend.*

●In separate dish put **TWO** ingredients. Blend with a fork and set aside.

●In mixer bowl put **THREE** ingredients, *room temperature.* Whip with whisk attachment on high about 5 minutes, until peaks are stiff and start to lose their shine.

●Reduce speed to Low/Stir and add liquids, then add dry ingredients by spoonsful, stopping mixer when all are added. Remove bowl from stand and give whisk a shake to dislodge clinging batter and egg whites into the bowl. Stir the batter with a large spoon until just blended, then scoop into a well-greased bread pan.

●Set pan in cold oven, turn on oven light and let rise for 1 hour. Leaving pan in place, turn on oven to 375° F and bake 25-30 minutes, or until internal temperature is about 200° F.

INDEX

Also by Em Elless —

The original minute-muffin cookbook for weight loss, diabetic & gluten-free diets.

Ready to eat in

One-two-three

minutes!

Dozens and dozens of single-serving recipes bundled into a banquet of nutritious breads and muffins – as low as 0 net carbs! From Sweet to Savory to Meals in a Muffin, these innovative mix-in-a-mug recipes are quick to prepare and only moments away from fresh-baked and ready to enjoy.

Savory Stuffin' Muffins rich with sautéed onions and celery, buoyant sandwich and hot-dog buns, Parmesan Salsa or Italian Herb, Banana Nut Bread or Strawberry Shortcake, Ricotta Comfort dinner rolls, Red Velvet with cream cheese, Maple Bacon for breakfast, a Reuben Melt for lunch- for starters! When you are in a hurry and want a hot nutritious low-carb meal or snack in minutes, this practical book will be your best friend!

About the Author

Em Elless has been creating recipes "for decades," but did not pursue a low-carb lifestyle until she learned she was borderline diabetic. "After all those years of following the latest expert diet rules – low-fat and six to eleven servings from the starch group each day! – I gained decades of pounds." She needed to make serious lifestyle changes but it was difficult and time consuming finding products that did not have hidden sugars or that relied heavily on refined white flours and other high carb ingredients.

"I worked full time as a professional artist and like most people short on time I wanted recipes I could whip up in a minute, ready to eat a minute later." She found a few "minute muffins" online but each recipe was basically the same with little variation. So her quest for creating low-carb breads and muffins began. She happily discovered that the most nutrient-rich foods also contain powerful antioxidants and little-known health benefits. She also learned that many gluten-free products contain high levels of refined starches which almost immediately convert to insulin – the fat-storing hormone. "Gluten-free dieters can enjoy many low-carb foods, but low-carbers can't eat most gluten-free breads. Up until now, low-carb gluten-free has been an oxymoron."

"Somewhere during this educational wake-up, my life's primary focus changed from art to developing low-carb nutrient-rich interpretations - not just substitutes - of their "refined" counterparts, without the bleached, starchy destructive ingredients."

After the successful launch of "Muffins to Slim By" in January, 2013, she turned to researching and testing yeast bread recipes, resulting in the breakthrough cookbook, "Low Carb Gluten-Free Yeast Bread Recipes to Slim By." She is currently exploring recipes for Volume 3 of the "To Slim By" series, the title and topic to be announced in mid-2014.

NOTES

_____

_____

_____

_____

_____

_____

_____

_____

_____

_____

_____

_____

_____

_____

_____

_____

_____

_____

_____

_____

_____

_____

_____